THE IDEOLOGICAL STRUGGLE FOR PAKISTAN

HERBERT & JANE DWIGHT WORKING GROUP ON ISLAMISM AND THE INTERNATIONAL ORDER

THE IDEOLOGICAL STRUGGLE FOR PAKISTAN

Ziad Haider

HOOVER INSTITUTION PRESS
Stanford University   Stanford, California

www.hoover.org

Hoover Institution Press Publication No. 584

Hoover Institution at Leland Stanford Junior University, Stanford, California, 94305-6010

First printing 2010
16   15   14   13   12   11   10   9   8   7   6   5   4   3   2   1

Manufactured in the United States of America

The paper used in this publication meets the minimum Requirements of the American National Standard for Information Sciences—Permanence of Paper for Printed Library Materials, ANSI/NISO Z39.48-1992. ♾

Cataloging-in-Publication Data is available from Library of Congress.
ISBN 978-0-8179-1085-3 (pbk.)
ISBN 978-0-7179-1086-0 (e-book)

The Hoover Institution gratefully acknowledges
the following individuals and foundations
for their significant support of the

HERBERT AND JANE DWIGHT WORKING GROUP
ON ISLAMISM AND THE INTERNATIONAL ORDER

Herbert and Jane Dwight
Stephen Bechtel Foundation
Lynde and Harry Bradley Foundation
Mr. and Mrs. Clayton W. Frye Jr.
Lakeside Foundation

CONTENTS

Foreword

FOR DECADES, the themes of the Hoover Institution have revolved around the broad concerns of political and economic and individual freedom. The cold war that engaged and challenged our nation during the twentieth century guided a good deal of Hoover's work, including its archival accumulation and research studies. The steady output of work on the communist world offers durable testimonies to that time and struggle. But there is no repose from history's exertions, and no sooner had communism left the stage of history than a huge challenge arose in the broad lands of the Islamic world. A brief respite, and a meandering road, led from the fall of the Berlin Wall on 11/9 in 1989 to 9/11. Hoover's newly launched project, the Herbert and Jane Dwight Working Group on

Islamism and the International Order, is our contribution to a deeper understanding of the struggle in the Islamic world between order and its nemesis, between Muslims keen to protect the rule of reason and the gains of modernity, and those determined to deny the Islamic world its place in the modern international order of states. The United States is deeply engaged, and dangerously exposed, in the Islamic world, and we see our working group as part and parcel of the ongoing confrontation with the radical Islamists who have declared war on the states in their midst, on American power and interests, and on the very order of the international state system.

The Islamists are doubtless a minority in the world of Islam. But they are a determined breed. Their world is the Islamic emirate, led by self-styled "emirs and mujahedeen in the path of God" and legitimized by the pursuit of the caliphate that collapsed with the end of the Ottoman Empire in 1924. These masters of terror and their foot soldiers have made it increasingly difficult to integrate the world of Islam into modernity. In the best of worlds, the entry of Muslims into modern culture and economics would have presented difficulties of no small consequence: the strictures on women, the legacy of humiliation and self-pity, the outdated educational systems, and an explosive demography that is forever at war with social and economic gains. But the borders these warriors of the faith have erected between Islam and "the other" are particularly forbidding. The lands of Islam were the lands of a crossroads civilization, trading routes and mixed populations. The Islamists have waged war, and a brutally effective one it has to be conceded, against that civilizational inheritance. The leap into the modern world economy as attained by China and India in recent years will be virtually impossible in a culture that feeds off belligerent self-pity, and endlessly calls for wars of faith.

The war of ideas with radical Islamism is inescapably central to this Hoover endeavor. The strategic context of this clash, the landscape of that Greater Middle East, is the other pillar. We face three layers of danger in the heartland of the Islamic world: states that have succumbed to the sway of terrorists in which state authority no longer exists (Afghanistan, Somalia, and Yemen), dictatorial regimes that suppress their people at home and pursue deadly weapons of mass destruction and adventurism abroad (Iraq under Saddam Hussein, the Iranian theocracy), and "enabler" regimes, such as the ones in Egypt and Saudi Arabia, which export their own problems with radical Islamism to other parts of the Islamic world and beyond. In this context, the task of reversing Islamist radicalism and of reforming and strengthening the state across the entire Muslim world—the Middle East, Africa, as well as South, Southeast, and Central Asia—is the greatest strategic challenge of the twenty-first century. The essential starting point is detailed knowledge of our enemy.

Thus, the working group will draw on the intellectual resources of Hoover and Stanford and on an array of scholars and practitioners from elsewhere in the United States, from the Middle East, and the broader world of Islam. The scholarship on contemporary Islam can now be read with discernment. A good deal of it, produced in the immediate aftermath of 9/11, was not particularly deep and did not stand the test of time and events. We, however, are in the favorable position of a "second generation" assessment of that Islamic material. Our scholars and experts can report, in a detailed, authoritative way, on Islam within the Arabian Peninsula, on trends within Egyptian Islam, on the struggle between the Kemalist secular tradition in Turkey, and on the new Islamists, particularly the fight for the loyalty of European Islam between these who accept the canon, and the discipline, of modernism and those who don't.

Arabs and Muslims need not be believers in American exceptionalism, but our hope is to engage them in this contest of ideas. We will not necessarily aim at producing primary scholarship, but such scholarship may materialize in that our participants are researchers who know their subjects intimately. We see our critical output as essays accessible to a broader audience, primers about matters that require explication, op-eds, writings that will become part of the public debate, and short, engaging books that can illuminate the choices and the struggles in modern Islam.

We see this endeavor as a faithful reflection of the values that animate a decent, moderate society. We know the travails of modern Islam, and this working group will be unsparing in depicting them. But we also know that the battle for modern Islam is not yet lost, that there are brave men and women fighting to retrieve their faith from the extremists. Some of our participants will themselves be intellectuals and public figures who have stood up to the pressure. The working group will be unapologetic about America's role in the Muslim world. A power that laid to waste religious tyranny in Afghanistan and despotism in Iraq, that came to the rescue of the Muslims in the Balkans when they appeared all but doomed, has given much to those burdened populations. We haven't always understood Islam and Muslims—hence this inquiry. But it is a given of the working group that the pursuit of modernity and human welfare, and of the rule of law and reason, in Islamic lands is the common ground between America and contemporary Islam.

A CONCERN WITH THE ideological and strategic challenge of Islamism, and with the U.S. security predicament in the Islamic world, must by necessity take up the question of Pakistan. After Indonesia, this is Islam's second-most populous nation-state that emerged from the partition of India in 1947, driven by the passion for a Muslim polity. With Iran knocking at the doors of the nuclear club, Pakistan is the Muslim state already equipped with nuclear weapons. Pakistan, then, is a conundrum. It has a gifted bureaucratic and judiciary elite, a massive army, and a middle class of perhaps fifty million people eager to safeguard the country's modernist inheritance. But it is also plagued with corruption, handicapped by an educational system that is a checkerboard of modern and religious schools, and broad swaths of its territory in Baluchistan and the Federally Administered Tribal Areas given over to banditry and terrorists from Pakistan and beyond.

In this essay, Ziad Haider, a young scholar of Pakistani background, keenly assesses the struggle for Pakistan's identity in a luminous account. He knows Pakistan deeply, tracing its ideological trajectory from its birth in 1947 through the secular, modernist ideas of its founders and then the steady erosion of that consensus in the 1980s and 1990s. He depicts a state that is ideologically adrift but he does not succumb to the panic and simplifications of so much writing on Pakistan today. As America makes its way—and pays the price in blood and treasure—in that "AfPak theater" in Afghanistan and Pakistan, we need a deeper understanding of both countries. This portrait of Pakistan is a valuable contribution to that endeavor.

Fouad Ajami
Senior Fellow, Hoover Institution
Co-chairman, Herbert and Jane Dwight Working Group on Islamism and the International Order

THE IDEOLOGICAL STRUGGLE FOR PAKISTAN

ZIAD HAIDER

SINCE ITS ESTABLISHMENT, the Islamic Republic of Pakistan has had three major fault lines that have underpinned its insecurity and that must be carefully navigated to ensure its future stability and prosperity: civil-military relations, ethnic fissures, and Islamic ideology. This essay is about ideology. It provides a political and cultural understanding of the role and use of Islam in Pakistan's evolution. Such a holistic understanding must guide domestic and international efforts to strengthen Pakistan as a modern state at peace with itself and its neighbors and to address the pervasive extremism poisoning it and posing a global threat. Pakistan's viability as a state depends in large part

1

on its ability to develop a new and progressive Islamic narrative.

THE IDEA OF PAKISTAN

From its inception in 1947, the idea of Pakistan was a contested ideological matter. Having lost their privileged status when the British supplanted India's Mughal rulers, Indian Muslims divided in response to a deepening cultural and political insecurity under colonial rule. Culturally, a schism emerged between the *Aligarh* tradition, which balanced selectively embracing Western notions of modernity and learning with retaining an Islamic identity, and the *Deoband* tradition, which rejected Western mores as a deviation from religious orthodoxy. Politically, as the independence struggle gained momentum, Indian Muslims divided into three primary groups. The first was affiliated with the Indian Congress Party, which advocated territorial nationalism. The second was affiliated with the All-India Muslim League led by Muhammad Ali Jinnah, which contended that Muslims had a special identity that would be erased in a Hindu-majority India—an argument that evolved from calls for political safeguards and a federation to an eventual demand for a separate Muslim homeland. The third included the religious parties that opposed a separate Muslim homeland to avoid dividing the Muslim *ummah* yet shared the Muslim League's concerns. Ultimately, the Muslim League prevailed and Pakistan was carved out of the subcontinent.

The irony of the dedicated struggle for Pakistan, however, was the ambiguity over the end goal. Indeed, one prominent South Asia historian, Ayesha Jalal, has argued that the lack of consensus over Pakistan's ideological and territorial contours was vital to its establishment: "Jinnah's resort to religion was not an ideology to which he was ever committed or even a device to use against rival communities; it was simply a way of giving a semblance of unity and solidity to his divided Muslim constituents. Jinnah needed a demand that was specifically ambiguous and imprecise to command general support, something specifically Muslim though

3

unspecific in every other respect. The intentionally obscure cry for a 'Pakistan' was contrived to meet this requirement."[1] This ambiguity played out in the pivotal 1945–46 elections in which the Muslim League was able to demonstrate that it was the sole representative of India's Muslims and Jinnah the sole spokesman. Jinnah and many of the Muslim League's leaders, though secular in their personal orientation, invoked Islam to make their case for an undefined Pakistan to Muslim voters, partly catering to pressure from their own coalition: "If you want Pakistan, vote for the [Muslim] League candidates. If we fail to realize our duty today . . . Islam will be vanquished from India."[2]

Proponents of Jinnah's secular vision for Pakistan often point to his eloquent speech delivered before the Constituent Assembly three days before independence on August 11, 1947: "You are free, free to go to your temples; you are free to go to your mosques or to any other places of worship in this state of Pakistan. You may belong to any religion or caste or creed that has nothing to do with the business of the state. . . . In the course of time Hindus would cease to be Hindus and Muslims would cease to be Muslims, not in the religious sense, because that is the personal faith of each individual, but in the political sense as citizens of the State."[3] The speech's inclusive message, however, has been diluted with time. Subsequent official accounts of Jinnah's life have included only edited versions of the speech with references to religion having no role in the business of the state being deleted.[4]

Yet the climax of this ideological debate in Pakistan's nascent days was the passage of the Objectives Resolution in 1949. The Resolution laid out the principles for Pakistan's future constitution, notably calling for a state wherein "the principles of democracy, freedom, equality, and tolerance as enunciated by Islam shall be fully observed" and "the Muslims shall be enabled to order their lives in the individual and collective spheres in accordance with the teachings and requirements of Islam as set out in the Holy Quran and Sunnah."[5] The Resolution thus injected religion into the core of Pakistan. Such a formal association between Islam and Pakistan was in many ways natural; however, it was the subsequent manipulation and distortion of religion for political and strategic ends that sadly emerges as a central theme in Pakistan's Islamic narrative.

In reflecting on the rampant religious extremism and sectarianism wracking Pakistan today, many liberal Pakistani commentators wistfully point to how far Pakistan has deviated from Jinnah's original vision as articulated before the Constituent Assembly. There is clear comfort and utility in remembering Jinnah's words as a guiding star in troubled times. Nonetheless, despite his personal beliefs and pivotal role as *Quaid-e-Azam* (Great Leader), Jinnah was ultimately part of a movement that was shaped by circumstances and alliances— one that evolved from fashioning an equitable postcolonial constitutional arrangement for India's Muslims to securing an independent nation. Indeed, throughout the movement, there never was a uniform vision of Pakistan or the role of Islam. Pakistan was and remains a product of contesting visions.

~

FORTIFYING A NATION

Upon achieving independence, Pakistan's leadership was faced with the daunting task of defending and consolidating a fragmented state against real and perceived external and internal threats. Emerging from the ravages of Partition, Pakistan consisted of an ethnically fractured West Pakistan and East Pakistan divided by one thousand miles of Indian territory. Many Muslims had remained in India, undercutting the two-nation theory of Muslims needing a separate homeland. Looming over this ideological and territorial vulnerability was the conviction that an irrevocably hostile India was bent on unraveling Pakistan, as it continued to stonewall on the delivery of Pakistan's vital and due share of resources inherited from the British. It was in this atmosphere of insecurity that Pakistan's rulers embarked on the process of using Islam to fortify a nation.

An early manifestation of this was to leverage the notion of *jihad* in shoring up the country's borders. Squaring off against India over the disputed territory of Kashmir in the hour of their separation, officers in the Pakistan army involved in the Kashmir operation of 1947–48 invoked *jihad* to mobilize tribesmen from the frontier and send them to raid and seize Kashmir; the government in turn called on religious scholars to issue supportive *fatwas* or religious decrees. This was to be the beginning of a long-standing state policy of using religiously motivated proxies to asymmetrically secure political and territorial gains vis-à-vis a seemingly hegemonic India. As the Bureau of National Reconstruction—an intelligence and research unit under General Ayub Khan, Pakistan's first military ruler—put it in 1963: "In its manpower, Pakistan is very fortunate. In some of the regions, people have long traditions of irregular fighting. Now that they have got a homeland and a state based on their own ideology they are bound to show great courage and determination to defend them."[6]

The notion of *jihad* has historic roots in Pakistan's frontier in particular. In *Partisans of Allah: Jihad in South Asia*, Ayesha Jalal describes the *Deoband*-inspired Sayyid Ahmad's *jihad* against the Sikh empire in his quest for an Islamic state in the northern areas as a landmark event.[7] In the early days of Pakistan, the army—though defined by a secular British military tradition—tapped these *jihadi* sentiments as part of its campaigns. Unsuccessful in wresting away Kashmir in 1948, the army again sent in irregular forces into Kashmir in 1965 only to fight an all-out war resulting in a stalemate. The war was rife with Islamic sentiment, as an officer of the Inter-Services Public Relations wrote: "There was a spurt of gallantry stories, of divine help, of superhuman resistance and of unrivalled professional excellence in the face of overwhelming odds. . . . The story of the suicide squad—a band of dedicated soldiers who acted as live land mines to blow up the advancing Indian tanks in Sialkot—became one of the most popular war legends."[8]

Just as Islam was leveraged in response to the external threat of India, it was also used to tackle internal challenges, from discrediting political adversaries to unifying a divided nation. As early as 1953, Jinnah's vision of a pluralistic Pakistan was challenged by street protests calling for a declaration that *Ahmadis*—followers of an alleged nineteenth-century messiah called Mirza Ghulam Ahmed —were non-Muslims. The protests were orchestrated in part to destabilize the federal government by calling for the resignation of Pakistan's first foreign minister, Sir Zafarullah Khan, who was an *Ahmadi*.

It was in this explosive milieu that the 1954 Munir Report, authored by two justices of the Federal Court, was issued sounding perhaps the most farsighted and eloquent warning about the nascent nation's ideologically destructive tendencies. Calling on the government to refrain from declaring *Ahmadis* as non-Muslims, the report cautioned against the notion that Pakistan was an Islamic state and that the state should define who is a Muslim; this would only foment charges of apostasy, divide the nation, and be inconsistent with Jinnah's vision of an inclusive polity: "The result of this part of inquiry, however, has been anything but satisfactory and if considerable confusion exists in the minds of our *ulama* [religious scholars] on such a simple matter, one can easily imagine what the differences on more complicated matters will be. . . . Keeping in view the several different definitions given by the *ulama*, need we make any comment except that no two learned divines are agreed on this fundamental. If we attempt our own definition as each learned divine has done and that definition differs from that given by all others, we unanimously go out of the fold of Islam. And if we adopt the definition given by any one of the *ulama*, we remain Muslims according to the view of that *alim*, but *kafirs* [unbelievers] according to the definitions of everyone else."[9] These words were to fall on deaf ears; in 1974, *Ahmadis* were officially declared non-Muslims through a constitutional amendment.

In a similar strain, during the first indirect presidential elections held under Ayub Khan in 1965, Khan's allies sought to discredit his primary adversary, Fatimah Jinnah—the sister of Pakistan's founder—by having a *fatwa* issued that Islam did not allow a female head of state—a refrain that would be echoed decades later vis-à-vis Benazir Bhutto—Pakistan's first female prime minister. Such attempts to Islamically delegitimize political players and segments of civil society—be it *Ahmadis* or later the *Shia*—has assumed an increasingly lethal undercurrent in Pakistan as many militants pave the way for killing their fellow Muslim citizens through *takfir* or declaring them as non-Muslims.

A more legitimate challenge, however, facing Pakistan's political and military elite was how to glue together a fractured state. For many, despite their secular orientation, the answer lay in the systematic promotion of an Islamic ideology as part of a top-down nationalist project.[10] Upon assuming power, Ayub Khan in a 1960 *Foreign Affairs* article spoke of his intention of "liberating the basic concept of our ideology from the dust of vagueness."[11] Elaborating in his autobiography on a peoples' need for an ideology, he stated, "they will have tremendous power of cohesion and resistance. Such a society can conceivably be bent but not broken. . . . Such an ideology with us is obviously Islam. It was on that basis that we fought for and got Pakistan, but having got it, we failed to define the ideology in a simple and understandable form. . . . The time has now come when we must get over this shyness, face the problem squarely and define this ideology in simple but modern terms and put it to the people, so that they can use it as a code of guidance."[12]

Yet the execution of this thinking was parochial, as reflected in the education sector. As taught in schools, the history of Pakistan was no longer a product of a postcolonial constitutional power-sharing struggle or the subcontinent's syncretic and shared Hindu-Muslim heritage, but an almost inexorable culmination of the arrival of Islam on the subcontinent. Notions of implacable Hindu and Indian hostility were reinforced, as reflected in Ayub Khan's own autobiography: "India particularly has a deep pathological hatred for Muslims and her hostility to Pakistan stems from a refusal to see a Muslim power developing next door."[13]

In a reflection of the continual contestation of the idea of Pakistan, Ayub Khan's vision of Islamic ideology did not go unchallenged. In the spirit of the Munir Report, Huseyn

13

Shaheed Suhrawardy, who briefly served as Pakistan's prime minister from 1956 to 1957, argued that an emphasis on ideology "would keep alive within Pakistan the divisive communal emotions by which the subcontinent was riven before the achievement of independence."[14] Instead, he argued for a Pakistan with "a durable identity between government and people derived through the operation of consent"—a vision that has yet to truly prevail.

IDEOLOGY AND INTEGRITY

Under Ayub Khan's military successor, General Yahya Khan, developing an Islamic identity for Pakistan's unity and defense remained paramount. Brigadier A. R. Siddiqui, head of military Inter-Services Public Relations, described the ideology and rhetoric espoused as follows: "Expressions like the 'ideology of Pakistan' and the 'glory of Islam' used by the military high command were becoming stock phrases. . . . They sounded more like high priests than soldiers when they urged men to rededicate themselves to the sacred cause of ensuring the 'security, solidarity, integrity of the country and its ideology.'"[15] Seeking to retain power, Yahya Khan utilized the intelligence agencies to orchestrate attacks by Islamic parties against the two major political parties—the Awami League and the Pakistan People's Party. Both were accused of being un-Islamic due to their secular and socialist beliefs. Suspicious of its own Islamic political allies such as the *Jamaat-e-Islami*, the regime even encouraged the emergence of other countervailing Islamic groups. As political and ethnic tensions boiled over in East Pakistan, the military launched a campaign that descended into a full-blown civil war with Indian intervention.

Once again, the war in 1971 was framed as a struggle for Pakistan's Islamic identity, threatened now by the Bengalis of East Pakistan, who though Muslims, were periodically depicted as corrupted Muslims and in collusion with Hindu India. As in previous wars, religious zeal was systematically employed to motivate soldiers and frame the cause. General A. A. K. Niazi, who led the forces in East Pakistan, invoked the "spirit of jihad and dedication to

Islam" that would enable the defeat of an enemy "whose goal and ambition is the disintegration of Pakistan."[16] The *Jamaat-e-Islami* was enlisted in East Pakistan in helping launch two paramilitary counterinsurgency wings. The enemies of Pakistan, according to Yahya Khan, were doing "their level best to undo our dear country[,] . . . a people whose life is pulsating with love of the Holy Prophet. . . . [E]veryone of us is a *mujahid* [holy warrior]."[17]

The 1971 war ended in catastrophe for Pakistan. East Pakistan separated, becoming Bangladesh, while nearly eighty thousand Pakistani soldiers became prisoners of war. Pakistani fears of India's hegemonic designs deepened; Ayub Khan and Yahya Khan's instrumental and parochial use of Islam to promote Pakistan's ideology and integrity failed; the rhetoric masked military interventions that weakened civilian rule, papered over legitimate ethnic grievances, and resulted in the loss of over half the nation. As in the wake of previous crises, an invaluable opportunity arose in the ashes of defeat to create a new national narrative.

ISLAMIC SOCIALISM

The task of defining this new narrative fell to Zulfikar Ali Bhutto—the first civilian politician to rule Pakistan after nearly fifteen years of army rule. Bhutto was a flamboyant aristocrat from the province of Sind, educated at the University of California at Berkeley. Having formed the Pakistan People's Party (PPP) only four years earlier, Bhutto ascended to power on a development platform embodied in the slogan "*roti* [bread], *kapra* [cloth], *makan* [house]." Like his predecessors at the helm of Pakistan, Bhutto had to wrestle with questions of Islam and ideology. Some contemporary commentators pointed out that the separation of East Pakistan had resulted in a more compact entity where Islam was presumably no longer needed to bind the state. Unity could have derived from a robust democratic process accommodating political and ethnic differences and looking toward "geological, geographic, ethnic, and historic grounds for regarding the Indus Valley and its western and northern

17

mountain marches as a distinct national unit separate from the rest of South Asia."[18] The Islamic parties however vociferously attacked Bhutto and his socialist ideology as a threat to Islam. Bhutto settled on the concept of "Islamic socialism" as his governing ideology to stave off his critics on the religious right and to create a new national narrative that promisingly leveraged core Islamic principles of justice, equity, and poverty alleviation to tackle a developing nation's fundamental socioeconomic challenges.

Yet with the passage of time, Bhutto's regime adopted a more conservative bent—a posture fueled by his insecurity vis-à-vis the military and his authoritarian tendencies. Bhutto introduced a ban on alcohol and gambling and made Friday a non-work day. In 1974, unwilling to stand up to street protests by the Islamic parties against *Ahmadis* and risk his government, he supported a constitutional amendment that declared *Ahmadis* non-Muslims. For the first time in the country's history, a minister for religious affairs was appointed to the central cabinet. Eager to burnish his Islamic credentials, in 1976, Bhutto invited the Imams of the Prophet's mosque in Medina and the mosque at the Kaa'ba—two of Islam's holiest sites—to visit Pakistan.

Bhutto's Islamic orientation was also reflected in his foreign policy. In 1974, Bhutto hosted a major Organization of Islamic Conference meeting in Lahore, reorienting Pakistan away from South Asia and toward the Middle East. Following India's allegedly "peaceful nuclear explosion" in 1974, Bhutto launched Pakistan's nuclear weapons program, rhetorically declaring "There's a Hindu bomb, a Jewish bomb and a Christian bomb. There must be an Islamic bomb."[19] In light of Pakistan's unsettled border with Afghanistan that divided a restive ethnic Pashtun population between both countries, the Bhutto government also began to support two Afghan Islamist militias to gain leverage over Kabul on the border issue: Burhanuddin Rabbani's *Jamiat-e-Islami* and Gulbuddin Hekmatyar's *Hizb-e-Islami*. The decision was to have far-reaching consequences. Both militias played a key role in the uprising against the Soviets; today Hekmatyar's *Hizb-e-Islami* remains one of the three key militant networks U.S. troops are targeting in Afghanistan.

Ultimately, Bhutto's promise of Islamic socialism was compromised by narrower political and foreign policy objectives as he failed to fully realize a new and progressive national ideology. In the wake of rampant street agitation led by the Islamic parties in conjunction with the intelligence agencies, he was deposed by General Zia-ul-Haq. It was Zia who would initiate the wholesale process of converting Pakistan to an Islamic state.

THE ISLAMIZATION OF PAKISTAN

General Zia's decade in power was a setback for a faltering democratic process and ushered in an era of religious obscurantism that affected every facet of domestic life and foreign policy. In his very first speech as chief martial law administrator after removing Bhutto from power, Zia, who was sincerely devout, described himself as a "soldier of Islam" and spelled out his vision: "Pakistan, which was created in the name of Islam, will continue to survive only if it sticks to Islam. That is why I consider the introduction of Islamic system as an essential prerequisite for the country."[20] As such, in contrast to Ayub Khan and Yahya Khan, who saw Islam as part of an ongoing and overarching nationalist project, Zia saw Islam as part of a revolutionary process to overhaul Pakistan.

The domestic impact was manifold. Beginning with the army, Zia, upon being appointed army chief by Bhutto, changed the slogan of the Pakistan army to "*Iman* [faith], *Taqwa* [piety], and *Jihad fi Sabil Allah* [jihad for the sake of God]." Officer evaluation forms included a box of comments on an officer's religious sincerity. Evangelical groups such as the *Tableeghi Jamat* linked to the *Deobandi* tradition enjoyed greater access to military officers and civil servants. Like his military predecessors, Zia cynically used the Islamic parties as a counter to his civilian political foes but also extended them unprecedented political patronage, initially appointing a number of *Jamaat-e-Islami* members to head key ministries. In the process, Zia also politicized other Islamic parties that had largely remained apolitical to date and empowered them. Along with separate electorates being introduced for non-Muslims, registration criteria that excluded most secular parties were introduced during elections.

Zia's Islamization also encompassed Pakistan's judicial system. The government constituted provincial *Shariat* benches at the High Court level and an appellate *Shariat* Bench at the Supreme Court level tasked with deciding if any parliamentary law was Islamic or not and whether the government should change them. Particularly troubling was the introduction of the *Hudood* Ordinance based on a distorted understanding of Quranic injunctions and introducing punishments such as flogging, stoning, and amputation (punishments that the state albeit never applied). The ordinance's most controversial application was and remains the imprisonment of female rape victims on the grounds of adultery. An effort was also launched to Islamize the education sector. In 1981, the University Grants Commission issued the following directive to prospective textbook authors: "to demonstrate that the basis of Pakistan is not to be founded in racial, linguistic, or geographical factors, but rather in the shared experience of a common religion. To get students to know and appreciate the Ideology of Pakistan, and to popularize it with slogans. To guide students towards the ultimate goal of Pakistan—the creation of a completely Islamicized State."[21]

The underlying motive behind these various genuine and cosmetic "reforms" was a moral zeal that animated Zia. Islam was no longer just an overarching ideology to harness to unify and defend the state; it was the road to salvation. Decrying endemic corruption and economic ills in Pakistan in a 1979 interview, Zia stated as follows: "In the last thirty years in general but more so in the last seven years there has been a complete erosion of the moral values of our society. . . . Islam from that point of view is the fundamental factor. It comes before wheat and rice and everything else. I can grow more wheat; I can import wheat but I cannot import the correct moral values."[22]

Under Zia a similar moral zeal characterized Pakistan's central foreign policy preoccupation in the 1980s: the Soviet invasion of Afghanistan. During Zia's rule, Pakistan became a staging ground for the insurgency against the Soviet Union, which was characterized as *jihad*.

In this effort, the Pakistani military leveraged the proxy Islamic groups it had backed since the 1970s, providing them with arms and financing in coordination with the U.S. and Saudi Arabia, among other states. Hekmatyar's *Hizb-i-Islami*, in particular, was a favorite of the Inter-Services Intelligence (ISI), which spearheaded the covert operation in Afghanistan. As an ethnic Pashtun, Hekmatyar was viewed as a potential leader under whom Afghanistan would be more favorably disposed toward Pakistan in the spirit of Islamic unity and less disposed to play the ethnic card. Ultimately, Zia's goal in transforming a limited Islamist rebellion into a full-scale *jihad* was to extend Pakistani influence into Afghanistan in light of its historic territorial concerns, secure significant assistance by helping the U.S. bleed its Cold War adversary, and allegedly "to make Pakistan the source of a natural Islamic revolutionary movement, replacing artificial alliances such as the Baghdad Pact." "This would be the means," continued one of Zia's confidants in describing his vision, "of starting a new era of greatness for the Muslim nations of Asia and Africa."[23]

In pursuing these strategic goals, the Zia regime with international aid systematically cultivated a virulent strain of Islamist ideology in Pakistan. The ISI made right-wing Islamic parties such as the *Jamaat-e-Islami* and *Jamiat Ulema Islam* key partners in recruiting among the millions of Afghan refugees in Pakistan and students at religious schools or *madaris*—lionizing those who volunteered as *mujahideen* fighting in the name of God. In the process, these parties developed extensive networks throughout Pakistan and deepened their influence. Students from impoverished backgrounds at the *madaris* were taught an obscurantist understanding of Islam with no modern subjects, making them easy prey for their handlers. Meanwhile, Saudi and United States funding directly facilitated this indoctrination. From 1984 to 1994, for example, the United States Agency for International Development gave a $51 million grant to the University of Nebraska-Omaha to develop textbooks filled with violent images and militant Islamic teachings as part of a covert effort to inspire anti-Soviet resistance.[24] Zia further opened Pakistan's doors to volunteers from all over the world who participated in the *jihad* in Afghanistan and who established offices, raised funds, and issued statements on Pakistani soil. Pakistan became the epicenter of a global *jihad* movement.

Alongside this *jihadi* culture, Pakistan under Zia also witnessed an unprecedented rise in sectarianism—once again triggered by both external and internal factors—which has claimed tens of thousands of lives in Pakistan. Externally, in the wake of the 1979 Islamic revolution in Iran, the Khomeini regime began exporting its revolutionary message across the Muslim world. Neighboring Pakistan became a battleground in a "transplanted war" between Iran and Saudi Arabia that sought to limit *Shia* influence—a struggle that violently played out among a hydra of sectarian groups.[25] On one side was the Iranian-backed *Tehrik-i-Nifaz-i-Fiqh-i-Jafria* (Movement for the Implementation of Shiite Religious Law); on the other were Sunni extremist groups such as the *Sipah-e-Sahaba*, ideologically equipped with *fatwas* issued by *Deobandi* seminaries in Pakistan and India declaring the *Shia* as apostates. *Sipah-e-Saha-ba*'s political demand was that the state should declare the *Shia*—15–20 percent of Pakistan's population—non-Muslims through a constitutional amendment, as done with the *Ahmadis.* Zia's support for the anti-*Shia* groups was largely in deference to Saudi Arabia. Not only was the Kingdom central to funding the *jihad,* but also it enabled Pakistan's initial acquisition of F-16s from the U.S., provided oil to Pakistan on a deferred-payment basis, and hosted a large number of Pakistan expatriate workers.

The cumulative effect of the Zia years in Pakistan was not just a wholesale Islamization of the Pakistani state to varying degrees but also the explosion of a *jihadi* and sectarian culture in response to external forces that were nurtured for political and ideological reasons. It was in the throes of this period that Pakistan's drift into extremism began.

IDEOLOGICALLY ADRIFT

Upon the demise of General Zia in 1988, Pakistan entered a tumultuous decade of political

instability, near bankruptcy, international iso-
lation, and a hardening *jihadi* culture—a period during which it remained dangerously
adrift.

The decade saw four consecutive democratic
governments—alternating twice under Benazir
Bhutto and Nawaz Sharif—come crashing
down before any could finish a full term. The
jostling among Pakistan's power troika—the
army chief, the president, and the prime minister—kept Pakistan at the brink of a political
precipice. Although Bhutto and Sharif's governments were discredited in large part by their
own corruption and malfeasance, as in the
past, the intelligence services in collaboration
with a range of Islamic parties and other elements undermined them and the democratic
process. The prime example was during the
1988 election that brought Bhutto to power.
During this election, the ISI-backed *Islami
Jamhoori Ittehad* (IJI) bitterly attacked Bhutto
on the grounds that Islam did not permit a
woman to serve as a head of state and that she
would be unable to safeguard the country's
ideological and national security interests.

Yet Pakistan's mainstream politicians were not immune to such manipulation either. In 1999, Sharif as prime minister tried to make *Shariat* (Islamic law) part of Pakistan's constitution. The bill passed the lower house and was slated to pass the upper house in 2000 when Sharif's party was expected to gain control of the Senate. Prior to that, however, Sharif was deposed in a coup by his handpicked army chief, Pervez Musharraf, marking the end of Pakistan's lost decade of democracy. During this period, no attempt was made to chart a new course for Pakistan as it swirled in a political maelstrom with stunted development, providing fertile ground for unemployment, illiteracy, and extremism.

Yet, in contrast to its internal political vicissitudes, Pakistan externally pursued a consistent policy of leveraging Islamic proxies against its neighbors to advance perceived national security goals. With the Soviet withdrawal from Afghanistan and the imposition of sanctions on Pakistan in light of its nuclear program, Pakistan entered the 1990s isolated, economically crippled, and, in its

29

view, abandoned by the United States with a *jihadi* corps in its midst. Many of these elements were redirected to Kashmir to wage a proxy war against India, hijacking the nationalist movement that had emerged in Indian-held Kashmir. Although Pakistan claimed to provide political and moral support to the Kashmiri struggle, the strategic rationale was to tie down Indian troops in Kashmir and bleed it by a thousand cuts in order to bring it to the table to negotiate on Kashmir. On the western front, keen to avoid at best a continuing descent into chaos in Afghanistan and at worst a hostile regime that might play the Pashtun card in Pakistan, the army, with the civilian leadership fully on board, began to back the military campaign of a new class of warriors that had emerged from Pakistan's *madaris*—the Taliban. Both in Kashmir and Afghanistan, the goal was to leverage Islamic groups to offset Pakistan's seemingly hostile neighbors—a policy with clear historical antecedents. Although the goals were rational, the means resulted in lethal blowback.

ENLIGHTENED MODERATION

With Musharraf's coup and alignment with the U.S.-led "war on terror" after 9/11, Pakistan once again arrived at a critical crossroads following a regional crisis. Forced to confront the specter of Islamic extremism in the international limelight, the country faced an age-old question: What was its Islamic ethos? Musharraf's answer was "enlightened moderation."

Beginning with his landmark address to the nation in January 2002 where he called for rejecting terrorism in Kashmir and combating extremism and intolerance, Musharraf throughout his time in power made his plea for enlightened moderation.[26] Enlightened moderation, as outlined by him, was a two-pronged strategy: "The first part is for the Muslim world to shun militancy and extremism and adopt the path of socioeconomic uplift. The second is for the West, and the United States in particular, to seek to resolve all political disputes with justice and to aid in the socioeconomic betterment of the deprived Muslim world."[27] Although Musharraf's

31

formulation was an important attempt to provide an overarching vision for Pakistan and to nationally delegitimize extremism, its execution was deficient and resulted in anything but moderation.

While taking some tentative steps in the spirit of enlightened moderation, Musharraf eventually faltered. Measures such as banning a number of key militant groups and beginning the process of registering *madaris* and reforming their curricula proved tentative: militant groups sprung up under other names, the registration process came to a grinding halt, and longstanding deficiencies in the public education curriculum remained largely unaddressed. Meanwhile, Musharraf's alliance of political expediency with the Islamic parties and ban of the heads of the two mainstream political parties—Bhutto and Sharif—resulted in a political vacuum that was filled by the Islamic parties and enabled the further flourishing of obscurantism in the country.

Moreover, while largely forward leaning in tackling *Al-Qaeda*, the army did not fully sever links with the Taliban or with a number of militant groups operating in Afghanistan and Kashmir, again in the interests of retaining strategic proxies. Compounding the challenge was that some groups such as *Lashkar-e-Taiba,* operating in Kashmir, had over time become part of the social fabric of Pakistan in terms of their perceived heroism in allegedly championing the Kashmiri cause and also in delivering critical social services, for example in the wake of the Kashmir earthquake. Moving against their erstwhile protégés at the seeming behest of the United States or India could trigger a public backlash.

In sum, Musharraf failed to successfully anchor enlightened moderation in Pakistan, largely due to policies that empowered the Islamic parties and tolerated militant groups. Militant groups that had once trained their guns across the border turned them inward and expanded their control in the frontier region through government-initiated peace deals; fiery clerics and vigilante youth squads who tasked themselves with enforcing Islamic morality proliferated in parts of the country, culminating in the taking over of the Red Mosque in Islamabad in 2007 and its storming by the army. As enlightened moderation dimmed, it gave way to a darker phenomenon: Talibanization.

TALIBANIZATION

Today, Pakistan faces an existential militant Islamist threat that its elected government is trying to combat in fractious collaboration with the army. Suicide attacks against army headquarters, to academic institutions, etc., reflect the critical threat the Pakistani state faces as these extremists strike at the hardest and softest of targets and instill pervasive fear and insecurity. Whereas once Islam underpinned the state's flawed narrative of nation building and strategic security, nonstate actors have hijacked that narrative with an extremist interpretation of Islam for a variety of motives, including the pursuit of a new Islamic order. It is this hijacking of the national Islamic narrative that is a defining feature of Pakistan's current troubles.

On one hand, there are groups that regard the Pakistani state as an enemy of Islam for having sided with the United States in the invasion of Afghanistan and applying force against them. The army remains locked in a struggle with the *Tehreek-e-Taliban Pakistan* (TTP), commonly referred to as the Pakistani Taliban, in the Federally Administered Tribal Areas (FATA)—once a staging ground for the Soviet *jihad*. The reach of extremism in Pakistan today, however, can only be fully understood by examining the presence of a multitude of establishment-spawned *jihadi* groups in the Punjabi heartland of Pakistan that are turning on the state. These include the *Sipah-e-Sahaba Pakistan* (SSP), *Lashkar-e-Jhangvi* (LeJ), *Jaish-e-Mohammad* (JeM), and *Lashkar-e-Taiba* (LeT), who thrive in southern Punjab amidst poverty and unemployment. Their recruits come from the more than three thousand *madaris* in Punjab, many of which have provided foot soldiers for the Soviet *jihad*, the Kashmir struggle, sectarian conflict, and now *Al Qaeda*'s terrorist operations in Pakistan and Afghanistan.[28]

Alongside these groups are ones waving the banner of an Islamic state and a return to religious purity as the antidote to the Pakistani state's inability to provide basic services, tackle economic inequities, and deliver justice. Their narrative is a direct function of state failure; their goal is a new if entirely undefined Islamic state—a struggle reminiscent of Sayyid Ahmad's *jihad* against the *Sikhs*. The conflict in Swat is a prime example where a longstanding movement for the implementation of *Shariah* law, fueled by anger at a broken system of justice and an exploitative landed class, violently boiled over with TTP support. Through a series of agreements with the government to cease fire in exchange for the implementation of Islamic law, militants steadily moved within one hundred miles of Islamabad, with one of the leaders claiming that democracy was not an appropriate system of governance in Pakistan. Although the military eventually rebuffed these groups, for the first time their territorial and ideological aspiration vis-à-vis the Pakistani state became clear.

Although the military response to combat these groups is well known and documented, the ideological response is equally important. Here the role of the Islamic parties and clerics is of particular interest. There has always been some tension among Pakistan's Islamic parties about whether to pursue their avowed goal of an Islamic state through democracy or insurgency. Although they have never gotten more than 12 percent of the national vote, and that during the Musharraf era, riding a wave of anti–United States sentiment following the invasion of Afghanistan, the Islamic parties continue to project influence well beyond their numbers. They have however largely bought into the democratic process and have periodically spoken out against the violent tactics of insurgents. Alongside the role of the Islamic parties in disavowing such violent means is the question of mounting an ideological defense and reclaiming, if not the narrative, at least a less radical understanding of Islam. The current government has attempted to do this by setting up of a seven-member Sufi Advisory Council (SAC) with the aim of combating extremism and fanaticism by spreading Sufism —a more peaceful and less rigid form of Islam

anchored in the subcontinent's history—
throughout the country.[29]

Currently, as the state finds itself on the defensive against an array of groups claiming to wave the banner of Islam, it must decisively counter their ideology. In doing so, it and the West must recognize that the core issue is not always a quest for Islamic purity but a reliance on Islamic rhetoric to mask more earthy concerns related to power, poverty, and justice that circle back to the need for better governance in Pakistan. At the same time, *jihad*—long sanctioned by the state for its strategic security reasons—to achieve these ends must be delegitimized. "It is time for the government to come out in public and explain the nature of the enemy," said Khalid Aziz, a former chief secretary of the North-West Frontier Province. "The national narrative in support of *jihad* has confused the Pakistani mind. . . . All along we've been saying these people are trying to fight a war of Islam, but there is a need for transforming the national narrative."[30]

YEH HUM HAMEEN (THIS IS NOT US)

To stave off the ideological inroads of extremism and generate a progressive narrative in Pakistan, the most important constituency is the people of Pakistan. In the Western media, Pakistan is often portrayed as a radicalizing society, caught between the mosque and military and teetering on the brink of fundamentalism. The reality is more complex. Pakistan has a robust civil society as seen in the recent lawyers' movement; its media is among the most prolific in the Muslim world. A moderate majority exists that rejects extremism and suicide bombing yet believes in the concept of a Muslim *ummah* and is anti-U.S. on a host of issues; that condemns the actions of the Taliban and their ilk as a distortion of Islam yet is uncertain about the means to counter them, particularly the use of force against fellow citizens and Muslims. Deep schisms exist among "moderate" Pakistani Muslims, tracing back to the divide between the *Aligarh* and *Deoband* schools pre-Partition—those who embrace religions and notions of modernity and those who seek salvation in Islam's perceived fundamentals. To understand Pakistan's Islamic ideology, it is vital to examine this not just at the state level but also at a societal level.

The pervasive strand of Islam among the subcontinent's Muslims has historically been *Sufi* or *Barelvi* Islam. *Sufi* Islam is viewed as more inclusive and flexible, paying no heed to caste, creed, ethnicity, or race. Its physical manifestation in the subcontinent has long been the plethora of shrines across Pakistan frequented by the masses seeking relief from living saints or *pirs* for their ills, though this insertion of a conduit between man and God has been ripe for manipulation. Since independence, Pakistan's *Sufi* culture has come under great strain due to internal and external reasons. Internally, successive regimes have co-opted influential *pirs*, who, in becoming increasingly politicized and prosperous, came to be viewed by many as part of the hegemonic socioeconomic order in Pakistan. Meanwhile, beginning in the 1970s, more conservative

Deobandi and *Wahabi* views gained greater currency based on four factors: the importation of this ideology by Pakistani workers who went to Saudi Arabia and the Gulf to capitalize on the oil boom; the embrace of these views by many in the middle class as Sufism came to be identified with a particular hegemonic order and the state's failings came to be viewed as only remediable by returning to a purer if amorphous form of Islam; the pan-Islamic revivalism following the Iranian revolution and Saudi attempts to ideologically counter Iranian influence, including in Pakistan; and the aggressive promotion of *Wahabi* and *Deobandi* thought in Pakistan during the Soviet *jihad* through a burst of Saudi financing, *madaris*, and state policy. As such, Pakistani society's complex Islamic texture has emerged from the top down and bottom up as a more conservative form of Islam has gained currency in a changing socioeconomic context.[31]

The ramifications of this can be seen in Pakistan today as encapsulated in the trenchant criticism of one Pakistani commentator: "In

Pakistan's lower-middle and middle classes lurks a grim and humorless Saudi-inspired revivalist movement that frowns on any and every expression of joy and pleasure. Lacking any positive connection to culture and knowledge, it seeks to eliminate 'corruption' by regulating cultural life and seizing control of the education system."[32] Indeed, over the decades, there has been an increase in conservatism ranging from more women taking to wearing the veil, music and dancing being viewed by many as un-Islamic, increased censorship in the name of Islam, and, in light of a defunct public education system, *madaris* churning out thousands of students who project a parochial moral zeal and fear far beyond their numbers. A pervasive austerity has hardened across Pakistani society.

Yet many Pakistanis are cognizant of the distinction between conservatism and fanaticism. One example of this was the strong support for a military response in the Swat Valley under Taliban sway in the spring and summer of 2009. This support was catalyzed by the release of a video showing a woman being brutally flogged by the Taliban—a video that provoked widespread public anger, highlighting the increasing power of Pakistan's media in shaping perceptions. Another powerful public rejection of Islamic extremism can be seen in the success of the movie *Khuda Ke Liye* (*For God's Sake*), released in 2007. One of the all-time highest grossing films in Pakistan's cinematic history (and the first to be screened in India in forty years), the movie was a powerful critique of both the distortion of Islam to extremist ends as well as U.S. policy toward Muslim-Americans post-9/11. A third expression is the *Yeh Hum Naheen* (This Is Not Us) movement in Pakistan, with billboards in major cities urging Pakistanis to reject extremism and claiming that Islam is a religion of peace. These expressions of civil society even when emanating from specific strata are important to consider in understanding the way ordinary people in Pakistan perceive the role of religion in their lives as well as its distortion. Indeed, a coherent consolidation and injection of such expressions into the national discourse are a vital antidote to the extremism coursing through the veins of Pakistani society.

A NEW NARRATIVE

From the very creation of Pakistan, Islam has been and will always remain a central social and political force. This report sought to paint a broad picture of how Islam has been harnessed through Pakistan's history for everything from nation building to strategic security—an enterprise that was radically escalated during the Zia era. The blowback of this is clear today. The Islamic narrative in Pakistan has been hijacked by an array of groups who use religion as a means to diverse ends: to secure political and territorial power, exorcise corrosive Western influence, engage in class warfare, redress perceived injustices, and even overturn the state in pursuit of a purer Islamic order. The use and understanding of Islam in Pakistan has always been in flux, evolving in response to time and internal and external events. The

44

question that arises, then, is not whether religion has a role in Pakistan but how it can be channeled as a force for progressive change. What form should an enabling narrative of Islam in Pakistan assume? Part of the answer lies in focusing on building an inclusive and robust Pakistani state invoking progressive Islamic values. The onus lies with the Pakistani leadership and people, but the international community can help in the promotion of good governance, education reform, and economic opportunity, as well as in the resolution of deep-seated regional insecurities and grievances that have led to the cultivation of extremist entities as a matter of state policy. The history delineated in this report provides critical context in this effort, but the report intentionally refrains from prescription or projection. Indeed, it concludes with the overarching lessons that Pakistan was and remains a contested idea and that embedded in every crisis is a vital opportunity to create a new narrative.

NOTES

1. Ayesha Jalal, *The State of Martial Rule* (Cambridge: Cambridge University Press, 1990), p. 16.

2. Khalid bin Sayeed, *Pakistan: The Formative Phase* (London: Oxford University Press, 1968), pp. 198–99.

3. *Quaid-i-Azam Mohammed Ali Jinnah's Speeches as Governor-General of Pakistan 1947–48* (Karachi: Government of Pakistan, 1964).

4. Ardeshir Cowasjee, "In the Name of Religion," *DAWN*, October 5, 2003, *http://www.dawn.com/weekly/cowas/20020310.htm*.

5. Ardeshir Cowasjee, "The Sole Statesman – 3," *DAWN*, July 2, 2000, *http://www.dawn.com/weekly/cowas/20000702.htm*.

6. Husain Haqqani, *Pakistan: Between Mosque and Military* (Washington, DC: Carnegie Endowment for International Peace, 2005), p. 46.

7. Ayesha Jalal, *Partisans of Allah: Jihad in South Asia* (Cambridge: Harvard University Press, 2008).

8. A. R. Siddiqui, *The Military in Pakistan: Image and Reality* (Lahore: Vanguard Books, 1996), p. 107.

9. Report of the Court of Inquiry constituted under Punjab Act II of 1954 to enquire into the Punjab Disturbances of 1953 (Lahore: Government Printing Press, 1953), pp. 215–18.

10. The following analysis of Generals Ayub and Yahya Khan's attempts to develop Pakistan's Islamic ideology draws on Husain Haqqani's cited *Pakistan: Between Mosque and Military*.

11. Mohammed Ayub Khan, "Pakistan Perspective," *Foreign Affairs*, vol. 38, no. 4, July 1960, p. 547.

12. Ayub Khan, *Friends Not Masters* (London and Karachi: Oxford University Press, 1967), pp. 196–97.

13. Ibid., p. 183.

14. Huseyn Shaheed Suhrawardy, "Political Stability and Democracy in Pakistan," *Foreign Affairs*, vol. 35, no. 3, April 1957, p. 425.

15. Siddiqui, *Military in Pakistan*, pp. 163–64.

16. Ibid., pp. 204–206.

17. Michael Hornsby, "President Yahya Dashes Hopes of Reconciliation," *Times* (London), July 3, 1971.

18. William L. Richter, "Political Dynamics of Islamic Resurgence in Pakistan," *Asian Survey*, vol. 19, no. 6, June 1979, p. 549.

19. "The Islamic Bomb," *Time*, July 9, 1979, *http://www.time.com/time/magazine/article/0,9171,920461,00.html.*

20. "General Zia ul-Haq's Address to the Nation on July 5, 1977." Quoted in Hasan-Askari Rizvi, *The Military and Politics in Pakistan 1947–1986* (Lahore: Progressive Publishers, 1986), pp. 289–93.

21. Stephen Cohen, *The Idea of Pakistan* (Washington, DC: Brookings Institution Press, 2004), p. 171.

22. President Zia-ul Haq's interview to Ian Stephens, January 6, 1979, in President of Pakistan General Mohammad Zia ul-Haq – Interviews to Foreign Media, vol. II (Islamabad: Government of Pakistan, undated), pp.

2–6. Quoted in Haqqani, *Pakistan: Between Mosque and Military*, p. 135.

23. Ziaul Islam Ansari, *General Muhammad Zia ul-Haq: Shaksiat aur Karnamay* [Man and His Achievements] (Lahore: Jang Publishers, 1990) p. 24. Quoted in Haqqani, *Pakistan: Between Mosque and Military*, p. 193.

24. "From U.S., the ABC's of Jihad," *Washington Post*, March 23, 2002, *http://www.washingtonpost.com/ac2/wp-dyn/A5339–2002Mar22?lan guage=printer*.

25. *Sectarian War: Pakistan's Sunni-Shia Violence and Its Links to the Middle East*, event summary, Woodrow Wilson Center (Washington, DC), May 2, 2007, *http://www.wilsoncenter.org/index.cfm?fuseaction=events.event_summary &event_id=231933*.

26. "Musharraf Speech Highlights," BBC, January 12, 2002, *http://news.bbc.co.uk/2/hi/south_asia/1757251.stm*.

27. Pervez Musharraf, "A Plea for Enlightened Moderation," *Washington Post*, June 1, 2004, *http://www.washingtonpost.com/wp-dyn/articles/A5081–2004May31.html*.

28. For more on militancy in Punjab, see Aysha Siddiqa, "Terror's Training Ground," *Newsline,* September 2009, *http://www.newsline.com.pk/NewsSep2009/coverstorysep.htm*.

29. "Sufi Advisory Council Set Up," *The News*, June 7, 2009, *http://www.thenews.com.pk/daily_detail.asp?id=181907*.

30. Jane Perlez, "Pakistan Attacks Show Tighter Militant Links," *New York Times*, October 15, 2009, *http://*

www.nytimes.com/2009/10/16/world/asia/16pstan.html ?_r = 1&hp.

31. See Aysha Siddiqa, "Faith Wars," DAWN, February 14, 2009, *http://www.dawnnews.tv/wps/wcm/connect/ dawn-content-library/ dawn/the-news paper/columnists/ faith-wars-yn.*

32. Pervez Hoodbhoy, "The Saudi-isation of Pakistan," *Newsline,* January 2009, *http://www.interfaith strength.com/images/Pervez.htm.*

ABOUT THE AUTHOR

ZIAD HAIDER is a J.D. and Masters in Public Policy candidate at Georgetown Law and the Harvard Kennedy School. He previously served as foreign policy advisor to Senator Chris Dodd, professional staff on the House Committee on Homeland Security, and as a research analyst at the Henry L. Stimson Center's South Asia program. He was an American Society of International Law Fellow at the Human Rights Commission of Pakistan, where he researched governance reforms in Pakistan's tribal belt. Haider has appeared as an expert commentator in *Newsweek*, the *Associated Press*, and *Al Jazeera* and has written in the *Asian Survey*, *Far Eastern Economic Review*, *DAWN* (Karachi), and *Indian Express* (New Delhi), among others. A Fulbright Scholar in Southeast Asia, he received his B.A. from Yale and is fluent in Urdu and proficient in Mandarin and French.

Herbert and Jane Dwight Working Group on Islamism and the International Order

The Herbert and Jane Dwight Working Group on Islamism and the International Order seeks to engage in the task of reversing Islamic radicalism through reforming and strengthening the legitimate role of the state across the entire Muslim world. Efforts will draw on the intellectual resources of an array of scholars and practitioners from within the United States and abroad, to foster the pursuit of modernity, human flourishing, and the rule of law and reason in Islamic lands—developments that are critical to the very order of the international system.

The Working Group is chaired by Hoover fellows Fouad Ajami and Charles Hill with an active participation of Director John Raisian. Current core membership includes Russell A. Berman, Abbas Milani, and Shelby Steele, with contributions from Zeyno Baran, Reul Marc Gerecht, Ziad Haider, R. John Hughes, Nibras Kazimi, Habib Malik, and Joshua Teitelbaum.

Index